TEXT BY BARBARA NEWSON

Look at East Anglia in colour

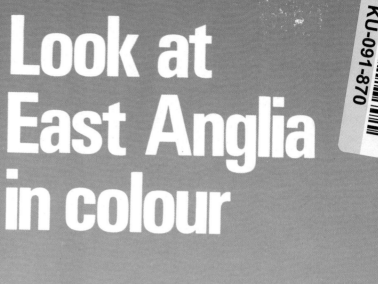

Introduction

East Anglia may be described as that long eastern peninsula bounded to the south by the estuary of the Thames and to the north by the Wash. It has no natural western boundaries. In earlier days, when man-made boundaries were concise, East Anglia consisted of only Norfolk, Suffolk, and the Isle of Ely; it was the land of the North Folk, the South Folk, and the Isle of Eels. Today man-made boundaries are not so clear-cut, but certainly when we consider the characteristics that Cambridgeshire and Essex have in common with the rest of the region, there is much justification for the modern trend of including them when talking about East Anglia. For this reason they are included in this book.

There is a general misconception that East Anglia is flat and boring and that it is not an area of fine landscapes. It is true that the East Anglian countryside is generally low-lying, but there are considerable portions far from level and there are many sudden inclines. There is also a great deal worth seeing. The rural scene usually predominates and gently undulating pasture, wooded hills, delightfully picturesque river valleys, and enormous skies present a constantly changing landscape to please the eye. It is a landscape which inspired a local school of artists, the Norwich School, as well as Constable and Gainsborough.

East Anglia is an area offering a great diversity of interest and appeal, and it may be said that there are really five distinct regions. By far the largest part is the fair-to-good arable farming country, which may be seen throughout the area. The Fens are also good farming country. These are a very fertile tract covering part of north-east Cambridgeshire, which was once wet marsh swamps and peat-bogs, and is now a prolific bulb- and potato-growing area. Another region is Breckland on the west side of Norfolk, and into Suffolk, a beautiful undulating region, with heathery moorland and forest. Also contained in East Anglia are the famous Norfolk Broads, some 200 miles of navigable rivers and shallow lakes, offering peaceful serenity and charming scenery. Finally there is the varied coastline with its popular holiday resorts.

Before the coming of the railways East Anglia was an isolated area, but now modern communications bring all parts of the region within easy reach not only of London and the South, but also of the Midlands and the North. People visit East Anglia for many reasons, not the least being to enjoy the dry, bracing climate. Visitors may come for a holiday on the Broads or by the coast, or for a sporting occasion such as golf, hunting, shooting, flying, or football. Specialists such as antiquarians, artists, naturalists, and architects come to find what they cannot see elsewhere. There is more evidence here in the villages, busy market-towns, and cities of the times before the nineteenth century and better preserved than practically anywhere else in England. Having had no such resources as coal, it missed the industrial wave of the nineteenth century which made the North Country great. On account of this there was no wide-scale Victorian development to obliterate the architecture from the great past when the wool trade brought wealth and prosperity to the area. As well as for its fine medieval, Tudor, and Georgian domestic architecture East Anglia is famed for the beauty and grandeur of its churches, the ruins of its abbeys and priories, and for its Roman remains.

For whatever motive one may happen to visit East Anglia, however, few fail to resist the curious charm of the area and many are drawn back again and again.

Norfolk

The wide arc of Norfolk's coastline is almost a hur
dred miles in length and within this is quite a varie
of coastal scenery. In the easterly section there a
long stretches of fine golden beaches, in the north
east there are gradually crumbling cliffs, while in th
north the receding sea has left salt marshes in i
wake. In this northerly part, separated from the sea b
these marshes and belying its name, nestles the litt
village of Cley-next-the-Sea. It is an old plac
it figured in 'Domesday' as Claia, and later became a
important port. Many of its houses and cottages a
built of flint along the narrow streets, and its pi
turesque windmill (1) dates from the eighteen
century and is a prominent landmark. West along th
coast from Cley is the quaint village of Wells-nex
the-Sea (2), which clusters round its church. It wa
once a thriving port and its harbour is still used b
fishing- and pleasure-craft, but Wells is nowada

4

more important as a popular seaside resort. Two miles
to the west is Holkham Hall (3), the seat of the Earl
of Leicester. This fine mansion in Palladian style was
built in the eighteenth century by William Kent for the
first Earl of Leicester of the first creation. It was his
great-nephew, the first Earl of Leicester of the second
creation, who also earned another title of 'Coke of
Norfolk'. Coke of Norfolk reformed agricultural work
in East Anglia, and Norfolk now leads the rest of
England in farming.

East Anglia is rich in splendid houses. Some fifteen
miles south-west of Holkham, is Sandringham House
(4), the private home of the Royal Family. The
Sandringham estate was purchased in 1861 by
Edward VII as Prince of Wales, and Sandringham
House, modified Jacobean in style, was built during
the 1870s. Sandringham has since then been the
home of four generations of English sovereigns, and
the original estate has been enlarged to approximately
20,000 acres.

Just south-west of Sandringham is Castle Rising
(6), where there are to be seen the remains of one of
East Anglia's perhaps most notable fortresses. The
fine Norman keep was built in the mid twelfth century
by William d'Albini and there is a great earthwork perhaps partly British and partly Roman work. In the
Middle Ages Rising was a port and a place of importance, but as the sea receded so Rising dwindled into
a village. King's Lynn (5), still further south-west, is
a pleasant old port close to the mouth of the Ouse.
King's Lynn has a history which dates back to Saxon
times, and during the Middle Ages was a walled city
of great importance. It is still a busy town and port,
and retains many reminders of its past, including the
two great churches, dedicated to St Margaret and St
Nicholas, the fifteenth-century Guildhall in Queen
Street, and the seventeenth-century Customs House.

5

6

9

7

8

Swaffham (7) south-east of King's Lynn, is a charming little market-town with buildings dating mostly from the eighteenth century or earlier. In the market-place stands the Market Cross, a domed rotunda surmounted by a statue, which was erected in 1783 by Lord Orford. Perhaps the chief feature of interest in Swaffham is the fifteenth-century Church of SS Peter and Paul. Its grand tower was completed in 1510.

Oxburgh Hall (8), a picturesque castellated mansion, is to be seen south of Swaffham. Constructed on a square plan and surrounded by a moat, it was begun in 1482 by Sir Edward Bedingfield. The house was passed down in direct male descent for well over four centuries and was given to the National Trust by the Dowager Lady Bedingfield in 1952.

10

11

Thetford (9) is an excellent centre from which to explore the interior of Norfolk, but it is also a remarkable place in its own right. Situated at the confluence of the Little Ouse and the Thet, it has an extremely long history, having been inhabited as early as the Old Stone Age. It was the capital of the Iceni, and during the eleventh century was the cathedral city of East Anglia. By the fourteenth century there were twenty churches and at least four monastic houses. With the Dissolution of the Monasteries Thetford's importance fell away, and it is now a quiet little town with some industrial expansion. Among the many reminders of Thetford's former splendour is the enormous castle mound, three churches and the ruins of a priory and an abbey.

South-east of Thetford, almost on the Suffolk border, is the pretty little market-town of Diss, standing round a large lake known as 'the Mere' (10). There are many lovely old houses in Diss, many Georgian or even earlier, and the Church of St Mary where John Skelton used to preach when he was Rector of Diss.

North of Diss is Wymondham, a busy market-town whose centre is the market-place. The charming Market Cross (11) is a two-storeyed, timbered octagonal building which dates from 1617. There are many interesting buildings in Wymondham. The most fascinating of these is probably the Abbey Church of St Mary and St Thomas of Canterbury with its two towers, standing towards the outer edge of the town.

Norwich is indeed a fine city, set in open and largely unspoiled Norfolk countryside, with forests, fields, broads, rivers, and the sea not far away. The city began with a Saxon settlement on the banks of the River Wensum, perhaps before AD 850; there are no Roman remains. By the time the Normans invaded it was important enough to be chosen by them as the site for a castle and a cathedral on the land between the rivers Wensum and Yare. This early importance was later reinforced by the development of the thriving worsted industry in the Middle Ages and Norwich was for a long time the largest provincial town in the country. In the nineteenth century the worsted manufacture declined, and Norwich fell behind in relative importance with the growth of the new industrial centres of the Midlands and the North. In due course other industries came to Norwich, and have given the present-day city a thriving economic basis. Such industries include shoe manufacture, electrical engineering, foods, printing, and many others. Industry is not the only source of wealth however; financial institutions also play their part. Among these is the Norwich Union insurance company whose business extends the world over.

Topographically the city has two centres. One is the former Saxon market-place of Tombland which

lies at the entrance to the Cathedral Close, while the other is the present market-place, which was formed outside the castle after the Norman Conquest. In Tombland is to be seen the magnificent Norman Cathedral (15), whose walls were built in stone about 1480. The spire is England's second highest. There is much fine work to be seen inside, including the Retable in St Luke's Chapel which depicts scenes from the Life of Christ, including the Crucifixion (16).

Not far from the Cathedral is Elm Hill (12), a restored medieval cobbled street leading towards that other centre of the city, the present market-place (13), which replaced Tombland as the city's trading centre in the fourteenth century. Behind this busy colourful scene stands the Church of St Peter Mancroft, rebuilt 1430–55, the largest parish church in Norwich. The Castle (14) looks down on to the market-place. Built on a spur of high land, the castle is covered with unusually fine Norman arcading, refaced about 1835. About 1890 it was converted into a museum, and is now one of the best in England. Notable are the natural history and archaeology exhibits, and pictures by artists of the Norwich School. From the Castle can be seen most of the ancient city churches; all thirty-two are worth visiting and several are magnificent.

14

16

Set among Norfolk's by-ways are many unspoilt and bewitching beauty-spots. One such place is Lyng Mill (17), a few miles to the north-west of Norwich and easily missed by the visitor driving to reach the coast or the Broads. Many holidaymakers do, however, visit the pleasant seaside resort of Sheringham (19) situated some miles north-east of Lyng Mill. The scenery is different here from that of the northern tip of the Norfolk coastline. There are no marshes here; the coast formation is of sand cliffs and remains so for many miles. At high tide the sea comes within a few yards of the cliffs and low tide reveals a sandy beach beyond the shingle. The holiday resort of Sheringham was developed in the late nineteenth century and early twentieth century, and above the resort stands the much older village of Sheringham. Both are set amid attractive countryside well worth exploring. The Broads are perhaps Norfolk's most famous attribute. Of these the closest to the sea is Horsey Mere, and the village of Horsey to the north-east has been flooded on several occasions. Horsey Church has one of the Norman round towers which are often to be seen in Norfolk, and the roof of the church is of thatch. Horsey Mill (20) has been very well restored and is a fine example of the windmills which were once numerous in Broadland.

Although the Broads are now used mostly by holidaymakers, they were once the thoroughfares for trading vessels. The wherry *Albion* (18), a fine example of these old trading craft, still sails the Broads, a reminder of those bygone days. The distinctive feature of such craft is the single black sail. The *Albion* was built at Oulton Broad and is now owned by the Norfolk Wherry Trust.

19

20

The ruin of St Benet's Abbey (21) on the River Bure near the Ant Mouth is perhaps the most remarkable landmark on the Broads. This Abbey was founded in 955 and after the Norman Conquest became one of the most important monasteries in East Anglia. The Abbey was abandoned during Henry VIII's reign and the fabric of the monastery was removed to build new houses. Today only the fine archway and fragments of walls remain. About 200 years ago a windmill was built into the ruins, but this is now itself a ruin.

Great Yarmouth is a port, a market-town, and a large holiday resort in a fine position by the sea and adjacent to the Broads. It stands where the Bure, Waveney, and Yare converge to seek their way out to the North Sea. It was an important town in Norman days, and some of its medieval town walls can still be seen. As a holiday resort Great Yarmouth offers almost every possible amusement and diversion, unrivalled golden sands, an extensive promenade, and two piers. The larger of these is the Britannia Pier (22) which has an amusement arcade and a large modern theatre.

Suffolk

24

25

26

27

28

Burgh Castle (24) stands in the north-eastern corner of Suffolk on the banks of the River Waveney. It was here in AD 47 that the Romans began their fortress, which they called 'Gariannonum', at a strong strategic position on what was at that time a huge estuary of the sea. Later it was extended to form a link in the chain of fortresses stretching from northern Norfolk down to Suffolk, Essex, Kent, and Sussex under the command of the Count of the Saxon Shore. The area enclosed is over five acres, oblong in shape with walls remaining on only three sides. These ancient walls have withstood the stress of wars, and tempests, and in some places are still fifteen feet high and eleven feet thick at the base.

The large seaside resort and fishing town of Lowestoft is the most easterly town in the British Isles. South Lowestoft has fine bathing beaches, while the harbour close to the town centre is an active and fascinating place with trawlers and other craft coming and going. Immediately west of Lowestoft Harbour is Lake Lothing and west of this is the most southerly of the Broads, Oulton Broad (25). Together these three form a continuous west to east waterway towards the sea. Oulton Broad has a very busy boating industry, and is the chief centre of speed-boat racing in East Anglia. In the summer season it is a particularly colourful sight.

Southwards along the coast from Lowestoft is the charming little seaside town of Southwold. From Norman times until the Reformation Southwold was a prosperous port, and then began to decline. In 1659 many of the houses were destroyed by fire and were not replaced by buildings but by greens which add a spaciousness in quaint contrast with the narrow streets lined with picturesque cottages. The attractive white lighthouse (26) built in 1890 overlooks the Sole Bay Inn at the heart of the town.

Thorpeness, further down the coast, was begun in 1910 as a seaside resort planned by Glencairn Stuart Ogilvie, an author and playwright. It was intended to be a quiet place and has remained so; one of the strangest buildings is the 'House in the Clouds' (27), a water-tower disguised as a house. Close by stands the windmill brought from Aldringham to pump water into the tower.

Two miles south is Aldeburgh, an attractive resort, once a shipping and fishing town until the sea advanced and eroded it. The old town was built on a level strip of ground immediately by the sea, and there is little remaining of the originally large town at this low level. The Moot Hall (28) which now stands close to the sea-wall, was built about 1520–40 and was once in the centre of the town. The more modern part of the town stands on the cliff behind the low strip. Aldeburgh has in recent years become famous as the centre of the Aldeburgh Music Festival, started in 1948 by Benjamin Britten.

29

30

31

The small market-town of Framlingham is one of Suffolk's treasures with its remarkable Castle (29), set on an artificial green mound, and its fine church. Legend has it that the site of the Castle was once a Saxon settlement. More reliable records tell that this site was given by Henry I to Roger Bigod in about 1100, and he built a fortified house, probably from wood. The house was rebuilt in stone by his son Hugh, the first Earl of Norfolk, and the second Earl, Hugh's son Roger, built the massive walls still seen today. Framlingham continued to go with the Norfolk title for many years, coming in the fifteenth century to John Howard, who was created the first Duke of Norfolk in 1483 by Richard III. The present title dates from that year. The remains of Framlingham Castle are impressive with the thirteen towers round the strong curtain-wall, enclosing an area of well over an acre. The Late Perpendicular Church of St Michael is a fascinating building containing much of interest including the late twelfth-century chancel arch, the fine hammer-beam roof of the nave, and the remarkable tombs of the Howard family brought from Thetford Priory.

Little Stonham (30), some miles west of Framlingham, is a quaint village with some lovely old buildings. Among these is the Perpendicular Church of St Mary which has a fine tower with a flint-panelled parapet; the nave has a double hammer-beam roof. West of the church is Little Stonham Hall, which is Georgian in style. The village inn, The Magpie, has a wrought-iron inn sign stretching across the main street, probably only dating from this century although it is said to have served the original inn of 500 years ago.

Saxtead Mill (31) on Saxtead Green near Framlingham is a fine example of a typical East Suffolk post-mill. The date of construction is not known, but must precede 1706, which is the earliest reference made to this mill. Saxtead Mill has been much altered, especially in 1854; it stands over a tall round-house and its machinery is of great interest. It is in the care of the Department of the Environment.

Woodbridge, south of Framlingham, is a pleasant market-town on the estuary of the River Deben. It is thought the Romans may have settled here, and there is evidence indicating a Saxon settlement in the vicinity. In 1193 an Augustinian priory was founded here, and in later years the town grew both as a ship-building centre and port. Now Woodbridge is perhaps most famous as a sailing centre. The main part of the town is set around the market-place and along the street called 'Thoroughfare' and Cumberland Street, where there are many lovely old buildings to be seen. Streets lead from Thoroughfare down to the quay where there is always an assortment of sailing-craft. The only remaining tide-mill, dating from about 1170, still stands by the waterside (32).

33

34

Ipswich is the county town of East Suffolk at the head of the Orwell Estuary, and is a busy, prosperous place, an important shopping centre, and a seaport. There is some evidence to indicate that the Romans lived here for a while, but little is known about those early days. After the Romans left, the Saxons built an important settlement here which they called 'Gipeswic', meaning 'the town at the head of the river', from which is derived the present name. 'Domesday Book' mentions Ipswich as a town of great importance and records that it then had nine churches. Later during the Middle Ages Ipswich was to achieve prosperity and importance through its wool trade. It became a prosperous port, built ships, and traded in coal. With the decline of the wool trade in the seventeenth century the town dwindled, but the nineteenth century saw it prosperous again with various industries. Ipswich today with its modern port is a thriving industrial centre, and its modern industries number among them engineering, fertilisers, and printing.

Ipswich is an attractive town retaining many interesting old streets and buildings. New developments at the centre of the medieval town are using many of the old buildings to great advantage with wide tree-lined terraces to provide an effect of spaciousness and light. Among the most famous of its old buildings is the 'Ancient House' (34), parts of which date from the fifteenth century. The house was largely rebuilt in the late sixteenth century, and in the late seventeenth century was refronted as it is seen today. It was occupied from the sixteenth to the nineteenth century by a family called 'Sparrowe', hence its alternative name of 'Sparrowe's House'. Silent Street (33) is a well-known Ipswich street, and its fine Tudor houses are typical of many with which Ipswich is still endowed. About five miles south of Ipswich is Pin-Mill (35) on the bank of the Orwell Estuary. It was once much frequented by smugglers, but now this pleasant spot is a haunt of sailors.

Woolpit (23) some miles north-west of Ipswich is an attractive old village with some fine timber-framed Tudor and Georgian-fronted houses. Woolpit has a particularly beautiful church dating from the fourteenth to fifteenth century, among whose treasures are a fine double hammer-beam roof, and some handsomely carved benches.

36

37

South-west of Ipswich, just inside Suffolk's southern border, lies East Bergholt famous for its connections with John Constable, one of East Anglia's greatest painters. One mile south is Flatford, a charming place on the Stour. Flatford Mill (36) was owned by Constable's father and was among the artist's favourite scenes to paint. Here too may be seen Willy Lott's Cottage (38) also immortalised by Constable's paintings, for example in *The Haywain*.

The picturesque little village of Kersey (37) in South Suffolk, has one main street which dips down-hill with timber-framed houses on either side to the small ford of the River Brett, or 'water-splash', at the bottom. It then mounts again between more lovely old houses to reach the church. Lavenham (39) in West Suffolk is one of the most charming towns in the country, rich in Tudor and Georgian buildings, and with little modern addition. Its famous church dates mainly from the fifteenth century.

38

39

40

41

42

The pretty little village of Chelsworth (40) stands beside the River Brett east of Lavenham. There are several lovely old houses; some of the finest are to be seen close by the eighteenth-century bridge at the east end of the village.

Newmarket is certainly the most internationally famous Suffolk town in horse-racing circles. It enjoys a magnificent situation amidst downs and heaths, ideally suited for the racing and exercising of horses (41). The town has more studs than any other in England, and is the centre of horse-racing in the British Isles.

Bury St Edmunds is a market-town, the county town and cathedral town of West Suffolk. In the seventh century it was known as 'Bedericsworth', and a monastery was founded here. In 869 Edmund, King of the East Angles died at a place called 'Haegelis-dun' and became regarded as a martyr. In about 903 his body was removed to Bedericsworth and the town was renamed and became a place of pilgrimage. Ruins of St Edmund's Abbey, founded in 1023, can still be seen, while the Abbey Gate still stands resplendent. The present Cathedral of Bury St Edmunds is the former Parish Church of St James (42), built in the sixteenth century.

Essex

44

45

Thaxted, set amid undulating countryside, is an ancient market-town, one of the most attractive in England. Before the Normans came there was a settlement here, and in the Middle Ages it became a prosperous place by weaving and the cutlery industry. In the seventeenth century the town began to wane, but Thaxted still retains many lovely old buildings in a variety of styles. The most imposing is certainly the late fifteenth-century Guildhall (43).

Finchingfield (44) is a charming sight, and is justifiably much photographed. The little Church of St John with its Norman tower surmounted by an eighteenth-century cupola is set on a small hill. The main street runs down the hill past the village green and the duck-pond, overlooked by charming houses of varying heights. Colchester is claimed to be Britain's oldest recorded town, and it seems that there really was a settlement here as early as the Bronze Age, about 1000 BC. In AD 43 the Romans invaded and founded the first Roman city in England here. After the Romans left, Colchester seems to have been of little importance until the Normans came and built a great keep here. In the Middle Ages Colchester prospered on the cloth industry, and during the Civil War was fought over by Royalists and Parliamentarians. Today it is the most important town in Essex, and retains many reminders of its long past. Traces of the ancient town walls still stand, and the magnificent Norman keep (46), is still in good condition, now housing a museum. There are several fine churches and many medieval buildings including the Old Siege House (45), a timbered building of about 1500 and marked by bullets during Fairfax's siege in 1648. East of Colchester on the coast are the popular resorts of Walton-on-the-Naze (47), Frinton, and Clacton-on-Sea, all blessed with good beaches.

46

47

48

49

50

South-east of Colchester, where Brightlingsea Creek joins the Colne Estuary, is the small fishing town and yacht- and boat-building centre of Brightlingsea. It is an ancient place with remains telling that the Romans were here. The grand Church of All Saints, a little away from the town, was built by the Normans and has Roman brickwork. Inside are fine brasses and monuments. In the town itself is to be seen Jacob's Hall (48) in the High Street. This timbered building was first recorded in 1315, and it is unusual in retaining a sixteenth-century polygonal stair turret. It is now a restaurant.

Mersea Island lies at the mouth of the rivers Colne and Blackwater, and is joined to the mainland by a road bridge across the Pyefleet. At the western end of the island is the resort of West Mersea (49) where there was a settlement in Roman times. There are now many modern houses, but the original village gathered round the little church retains much old-world charm and some of the atmosphere of its past as a small fishing and sailing centre. The Church of SS Peter and Paul dates from Norman times.

At Pleshey (50), six miles north-north-west of Chelmsford, there was once a great Norman castle on the mound which dominates the village, but it was already in decline in the fifteenth century. The name of 'Pleshey' is derived from a French word meaning 'an enclosure', and originally Pleshey was enclosed by a rampart and ditch, traces of which are still to be seen. Pleshey is a beautiful place with its cottages, Tudor house, fine trees, and its Church of the Holy Trinity, and is among the most famous spots in Essex.

Arkesden (51) is a pretty little village set beside a stream in a valley north-north-west of Pleshey. It possesses charming old cottages and farms, and the attractive Church of St Mary, parts of which date from the thirteenth century. Inside are a variety of ancient monuments.

52

53

54

Wicken Bonhunt just south of Arkesden is another charming old village, set amid fine countryside. The little Church of St Margaret has a thirteenth-century chancel although the rest was rebuilt in Victorian times. On the road from Newport to Wicken Bonhunt, at Bonhunt Farm a quarter of a mile east, is the complete little Norman Chapel of St Helen. In Wicken Bonhunt itself is the thatched inn, The Coach and Horses (52), which has an interesting sign.

Audley End, north-east of Wicken Bonhunt, is a small, predominantly Georgian village to the north of which stands the magnificent Jacobean mansion of Audley End (53). It stands on the former site of a Benedictine monastery, a site which at the Reformation was granted to Sir Thomas Audley. His grandson, Thomas Howard, was made the first Earl of Suffolk in 1603, and it is said that in the same year he began the new house of Audley End on a magnificent scale. The house seen today is apparently only a fragment of what was originally erected, but visitors can hardly fail to be impressed by this beautiful building with its mullioned and transomed windows, its many turrets and its elaborate porches.

North of Audley End is to be seen the little market town of Saffron Walden (54), a charming place with a long history. There was a Saxon settlement here before the Normans came and built a castle. In the Middle Ages Saffron Walden flourished on the wool trade, but in addition there was the saffron industry from which the town took its name. Saffron Walden is a complex town to explore, for it has two centres, the Market Place and the High Street, but many lovely old buildings survive to make it very attractive.

Cambridge
& Isle of Ely

e quiet country town of Ely stands on the eastern d of a spur of higher land, an 'island' in Fenland, d has given its name to the northern part of mbridgeshire. Although once the most important ace in the county it has never become large and is minated by its magnificent Cathedral. Ely has a long story, beginning somewhere about the mid-seventh ntury when Ethelreda, daughter of the King of the st Angles founded a monastery at Ely. This abbey as later destroyed in 870 by the Danes, but was ounded in 970 for the Benedictines. In the early elfth century a new abbey was begun to replace the xon one, and the abbot was made a bishop and e abbey church a cathedral. As the years passed the thedral was enlarged and beautified. The Monas- y was dissolved in 1539. Ely Cathedral (55) is a perb sight for miles, and on closer examination veals great beauties which should not be missed. Another place which should be seen is the city of mbridge, famous throughout the world. Cam- dge the City is older than Cambridge the University. e Romans and Saxons both had settlements,

Cambonitum and Grantebrigge, beside the River Cam. 'Domesday' records that Grantebrigge had about 400 houses and a Norman castle. The town flourished in its secluded position, and somehow a University began there in the thirteenth century, at first without any central organisation. By 1475 there were twelve colleges in existence, and by the Reformation fifteen. The first, Peterhouse, was founded by the Bishop of Ely in 1284. Since that time the Cambridge colleges have gradually evolved in an orderly pattern to meet the changing needs of students over the centuries. One of the great joys of Cambridge is that the city has retained so many open spaces. Rural charms in the centre of an urban area may best be appreciated in the Backs, the name given to the part of the River Cam immediately behind some of the leading colleges. One of these, St John's College (56) was founded in 1511 by Lady Margaret Beaufort, mother of Henry VII and architecturally its buildings give a representative picture throughout the ages. Perhaps one of its most remarkable features is the Bridge of Sighs (57), built by Hutchinson in 1831.

60

58

Southwards along the Backs is King's College founded by King Henry VI in 1440, and King's College Chapel (58) is the best known of the many architectural gems in Cambridge. It is one of the most important examples of medieval architecture in England and has been described as a chapel built on the scale of a cathedral. Inside it is 298 feet in length, 40 feet wide and 80 feet high, a building of great beauty with a superb interior. Perfectly proportioned it is rich and colourful with magnificent panels and carvings, and wonderful screens and choir-stalls. Although Cambridge is famous primarily for its University, there are other notable buildings unassociated with the University. Cambridge is the county town of Cambridgeshire, a busy shopping centre, and has some large factories although it is not an industrial centre. It is set in charming countryside with picturesque villages only a short distance away. Grantchester for example, well known through

Rupert Brooke's poem 'Grantchester' is only tw miles south-west of Cambridge by the river. Litt Abington (60) some eight miles south-south-east Cambridge stands close to the park of Abington Ha It is a pleasant little village, and with its thatch houses and cottages makes a charming sight. Church of St Mary has some Norman features and thirteenth-century chancel.

Linton some ten miles from Cambridge, furth along the road and set amid hilly countryside, is winding village set on both sides of the Granta. It h many fine old buildings, many of them Georgian. T Dog and Duck Inn (59) dates from the seventeen century. Linton is known for its village college whic was built in 1938. The fine Church of St Mary dat from the thirteenth century but its west tower an chancel are fourteenth century, and the north an south porches are fifteenth century. The church ch is one of the finest outside the Cambridge colleges